MARCH 50 COLORING PAGES
FOR ADULTS RELAXATION

SHIH CHIEN HUA

PUBLISHED BY:
SHIH CHIEN HUA
Copyright © 2018

SEABIRD SHOP >50FOR

FB FAN PAGE

Disclaimer
The information contained in this book is for general information purposes only. The information is provided by the authors and while we endeavor to keep the information up to date and correct, we make no representations or warranties of any kind, express or implied, about the completeness, accuracy, reliability, suitability or availability with respect to the book or the information, products, services, or related graphics contained in the book for any purpose. Any reliance you place on such information is therefore strictly at your own risk.

MARCH 1ST

note:

_____

_____

_____

MARCH 2ND

note:

_____

_____

_____

MARCH 3RD

note:

_____

_____

_____

MARCH 4TH

note:

_____

_____

_____

MARCH 5TH

note:

_____

_____

_____

MARCH 6TH

note:

_____

_____

_____

MARCH 7TH

note:

_____

_____

_____

MARCH 8TH

note:

_____

_____

_____

MARCH 9TH

note:

_____

_____

_____

MARCH 10TH

note:

_____

_____

_____

MARCH 11TH

note:

_____

_____

_____

MARCH 12TH

note:

_____

_____

_____

MARCH 13TH

note:

_____

_____

_____

MARCH 14TH

note:

_____

_____

_____

MARCH 15TH

note:

_____

_____

_____

MARCH 16TH

note:

_____

_____

_____

MARCH 17TH

note:

_____

_____

_____

MARCH 18TH

note:

_____

_____

_____

MARCH 19TH

note:

_____

_____

_____

MARCH 20TH

note:

_____

_____

_____

MARCH 21TH

note:

_____

_____

_____

MARCH 22TH

note:

_____

_____

_____

MARCH 23TH

note:

_____

_____

_____

MARCH 24TH

note:

_____

_____

_____

MARCH 25TH

note:

_____

_____

_____

MARCH 26TH

note:

_____

_____

_____

MARCH 27TH

note:

_____

_____

_____

MARCH 28TH

note:

_____

_____

_____

MARCH 29TH

note:

_____

_____

_____

MARCH 30TH

note:

_____

_____

_____

MARCH 32TH

note:

_____

_____

_____

MARCH 33TH

note:

_____

_____

_____

MARCH 34TH

note:

_____

_____

_____

MARCH 35TH

note:

_____

_____

_____

MARCH 36TH

note:

_____

_____

_____

MARCH 37TH

note:

_____

_____

_____

MARCH 38TH

note:

_____

_____

_____

MARCH 39TH

note:

_____

_____

_____

MARCH 40TH

note:

_____

_____

_____

MARCH 41TH

note:

_____

_____

_____

MARCH 42TH

note:

_____

_____

_____

MARCH 43TH

note:

_____

_____

_____

MARCH 44TH

note:

_____

_____

_____

MARCH 45TH

note:

_____

_____

_____

MARCH 46TH

note:

_____

_____

_____

MARCH 47TH

note:

_____

_____

_____

MARCH 48TH

note:

_____

_____

_____

MARCH 49TH

note:

_____

_____

_____

MARCH 50TH

note:

_____

_____

_____

www.ingramcontent.com/pod-product-compliance
Lightning Source LLC
Chambersburg PA
CBHW081606220526
45468CB00010B/2786